Dual Meanings or words

from *11*

There are four sections in this book, and each section covers a different dual-meaning question type:

1. **Two-Section Dictionary Definitions**
   Find a single word that matches two separate clues.
   102 questions in this section.

2. **Context Clue Sentences**
   Using the context of a word in a sentence, locate the correct meaning of this homograph.
   82 questions in this section.

3. **Sentence Dictionary Definitions**
   Find a word that matches two different dictionary definitions.
   20 questions in this section.

4. **Homograph Word Banks**
   Match the five clues to words in a word bank.
   80 questions in this section.

A homograph is a word that has the same spelling as another but has a different meaning.

Please be aware that some homographs may be pronounced differently when spoken but will still have the same spelling.

Homographs can appear in various questions types in the 11 plus examination.

If you are having problems with a question try thinking of the word/homograph as a noun or as a verb. This often helps in locating the correct word meaning. If you don't know what a noun and a verb are then look their definitions up in the dictionary.

Good luck!

Rachel Higgins
BA (Hons). PGCE (Dis). MA. (Ed)

Dual Meanings

Section 1 : 2-Section Dictionary Definitions

Look at the five possible answers. Choose one that fits with the first set of words and then make sure this answer also fits with the second set of words. For example:

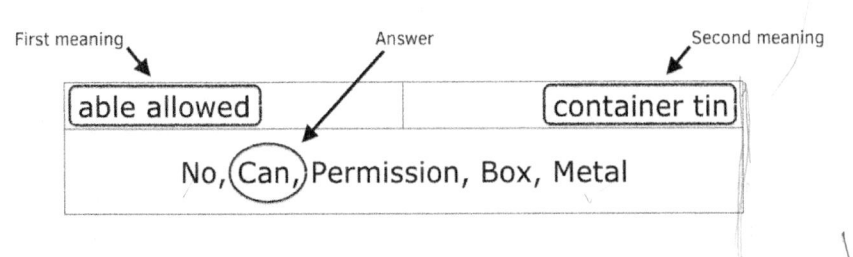

First meaning → [able allowed]   Answer   Second meaning → [container tin]

No, (Can), Permission, Box, Metal

Questions:

1. | water valve | light knock |

   (Tap), Cheap, Pour, River, Liquid

2. | short stroke | rushing movement |

   Feline, Line, Wrestle, (Run), Dash

3. | prevent flow | plant stalk |

   Tide, Stem, Hinder, Stop, Hyacinth

4. | round coil | current air |

   Cake, Button, Bun, (Wind), Back

5. | back garden | feet measurement |

   Hand, (Yard), Horse, Hoarse, Pound

www.11pluspass.co.uk — Page 3 — Copyright 2020 Rachel Higgins

Dual Meanings - Section 1

6	formal dance	object round
	Enjoy, **Ball**, Disagree, Action, Eider ✓

7	smell fragrance	anger enrage
	Praise, **Incense**, Nose, Annoy, Angry ✓

8	weaving machine	appear large
	Device, Apparatus, **Loom**, Shine, Threaten ✓

9	possible future	strength power
	Time, **Might**, Express, Great, Strong ✓

10	freshwater fish	complain fault
	Blow, **Tench**, Spring, Carp, Flaw ✗ Carp

11	ice pellets	call greet
	Hail, Shout, Sow, Ball, Echo ✓

12	purloin steal	cut notch
	Iron, Metal, Bandage, Hurt, **Nick**

6/7

Dual Meanings - Section 1

13	uppermost highest	outrank exceed
	Head, Skirt, **Top**, Great, Degree	

14	possession belongs	pit quarry
	Mine, Speaker, Colliery, Prey, Control	

15	box container	situation circumstances
	Trunk, Brief, **Case**, Site, Spar	

16	angry annoyed	sign mark
	Symbol, Medal, **Meddle**, **Cross**, Irritate	

17	astound stun	shake sway
	Gun, Wobble, Mass, Material, **Rock**	

18	firm tight	express hasty
	Quick, **Fast**, Soon, Abstain, Job	

19	register checkout	dig cultivate
	Till, Observe, Look, Crop, List	

Dual Meanings - Section 1

20. | tropical tree | hide take |

    Log, Type, Hand, Palm, Bay

21. | goat antelope | joke tease |

    Youth, Fool, Kid, Rib, Foal

22. | peddle sell | bird prey |

    Praise, Bicycle, Hawk, Scoot, Hunt

23. | guide direct | metal element |

    Plum, Lead, Plumb, Plume, Led

24. | fight spar | confine enclose |

    Contain, Fist, Ring, Duck, Box

25. | flavour spice | period time |

    Spell, Season, Watch, Chill, Taste

26. | side joint | stylish fashionable |

    Kneel, Design, Veal, Hip, Rose

Dual Meanings - Section 1

27. | utter communicate | fast rapid |
    Train, Express, Teach, Say, Prompt

28. | worktop surface | oppose contradict |
    Coin, Shop, Argue, Counter, Bench

29. | peninsula headland | poncho shawl |
    Crop, Cloak, Point, Cover, Cape

30. | perspective outlook | slant incline |
    Angle, Face, Slope, Binoculars, Direction

31. | levy tax | ring peal |
    Exercise, Pay, Toll, Platinum, Pear

32. | observe see | message reminder |
    Note, Leave, Bulletin, Shade, Line

33. | switch cane | weld bond |
    Premium, Baton, Push, Stick, Hold

Dual Meanings - Section 1

34	intellect brain	beware heed
	Crops, Watch, Wit, Peril, Mind	

35	loop tie	collection gathering
	Knot, Weave, Bow, Circle, Spiral	

36	racket paddle	flutter wink
	Oar, Bat, Club, Stick, Strike	

37	moment instant	mark indicate
	Quick, Spoil, Arrow, Fast, Tick	

38	missile bomb	crust shield
	Pie, Shell, Fire, Case, Mortar	

39	squash squeeze	conserves preserves
	Jelly, Wedge, Jam, Salt, Pack	

40	routine custom	addiction problem
	Solution, Miss, Pattern, Habit, Flaw	

Dual Meanings - Section 1

41	access entry	charm delight
	Lobby, Entrance, Ticket, Lucky, Angel	

42	positive concrete	company business
	Tarmac, Rigid, Friend, Firm, Dense	

43	gambol frolic	adventure antic
	Dance, Trip, Caper, Fall, Jump	

44	leg part	circuit tour
	Knee, Lap, Race, Lick, Splash	

45	granule crumb	pattern direction
	Cereal, Speck, Flour, Grain, Crops	

46	express state	sheer complete
	Utter, United, Quick, All, Train	

47	gash lesion	upset offend
	Hurt, Cut, Wound, Cry, Wind	

Dual Meanings - Section 1

48	single lone	underside shoe
	Only, Sole, Double, Horse, Engaged	

49	gaze examine	contemporary equal
	Stare, Look, Cut, Peer, Eat	

50	keyboard instrument	heart lungs
	Organ, Body, Trunk, Pipe, Part	

51	pale light	just reasonable
	Ice, Dark, Moon, Fair, Biased	

52	dull dreary	plane even
	Total, Runway, Flat, Odd, Smooth	

53	margin border	save invest
	School, Pool, Surround, Edge, Bank	

54	leaf sheet	call summon
	Elm, Page, Hollow, Duvet, Eider	

Dual Meanings - Section 1

55 | point end | spill empty
Finish, Tip, Gesture, Tilt, Head

56 | delay postpone | booth stand
Suspend, Stable, Pen, Stall, Safe

57 | battle contest | dash sprint
Race, Check, Colon, Imp, Comma

58 | trim wiry | bow bend
Slender, Loose, Stout, Lean, Arrow

59 | originate emerge | shade mark
Water, Hatch, Start, Jump, Shadow

60 | wane fade | bunting standard
Ensign, Baby, Faint, Flag, Model

61 | pummel strike | beat throb
Pound, Take, Mine, Saddle, Heart

Dual Meanings - Section 1

62	cruel nasty	imply indicate
	Mean, Pointer, Callous, Show, Unkind	

63	insert slip	nosh grub
	Worm, Hose, Slug, Tuck, Add	

64	source spring	glowing fine
	Luminous, Fountain, Fine, Detail, Well	

65	ashen pasty	fade soften
	Pie, Pale, Disappear, Pail, Liquid	

66	complain oppose	article item
	Protest, Site, Report, Object, Target	

67	elongated stretched	desire want
	Slow, Need, Linger, Long, Tense	

68	status level	rancid foul
	Even, Rank, Milk, Grade, Birds	

Dual Meanings - Section 1

69	airliner plane	spurt stream
	Fountain, Smooth, Jet, Spout, Air	

70	radiance beam	buoyant flimsy
	Heavy, Balance, Soft, Light, Feather	

71	support sustain	swallow allow
	Accept, Bear, Wild, Assume, Consume	

72	wallet case	queue line
	Row, Rasp, Purse, File, Column	

73	firm good	jingle noise
	Bell, Ring, Sound, Hum, Company	

74	omit miss	bounce prance
	Pass, Hop, Jump, High, Skip	

75	quantity amount	book tome
	Level, Volume, Straight, Section, Degree	

Dual Meanings - Section 1

76	cove inlet	howl bark
	Tree, Wail, Bay, Cave, Wane	

77	basic pure	obvious evident
	Raw, Bare, Plain, Ugly, Elaborate	

78	snarl growl	shout roar
	Yell, Bark, Trunk, Duck, Whisper	

79	orifice lips	entrance aperture
	Face, Stick, Mouth, Magic, Exit	

80	sheet folio	foliage flora
	Volume, Leaf, Fauna, Book, Root	

81	trace evidence	data note
	Paper, Monitor, Forensic, Record, Remark	

82	decorate adorn	floor level
	Punch, Cover, Deck, Dinghy, Board	

Dual Meanings - Section 1

83	foul disgusting	earn receive
	Gross, Owl, Minor, Awful, Collect	

84	fight quarrel	propel paddle
	Plane, Wrangle, Skull, Object, Row	

85	complain grumble	heifer meat
	Collect, Beef, Moan, Sigh, Veal	

86	dashboard instruments	committee board
	Truth, Panel, Team, Import, Dials	

87	rod cane	force team
	Staff, Cricket, Bat, Baton, Body	

88	guide coach	procession file
	Ring, Plane, Chain, Train, Bind	

89	glide skim	food fish
	Hook, Skate, Fin, Roller, Tail	

Dual Meanings - Section 1

90	variety breed	gentle humane
	Consider, Caste, Kind, Type, Caring	

91	status condition	nation land
	Declare, Shampoo, State, Ware, Country	

92	pursuit pastime	appeal fascinate
	Interest, Chase, Hobby, Fine, Attract	

93	even flat	jet aircraft
	House, Hobby, Black, Plane, Constant	

94	wilderness sand	leave abandon
	Beach, Desert, Beech, Discard, Dessert	

95	haunt follow	branch shoot
	Kill, Chase, Gun, Stalk, Stem	

96	mode category	font print
	Mean, Type, Letter, Key, Style	

Dual Meanings - Section 1

97	cuff blow	beat strike
	Puff, Punch, Wind, Sleeve, Note	

98	tug pull	bravery nerve
	Grasp, Hair, Junk, Pick, Pluck	

99	harass plague	domestic carnivorous
	Dog, Wipe, Locust, Fox, Wild	

100	circle halo	chime tinkle
	Clang, Hoop, Buzz, Ring, Sound	

101	apprentice scholar	eye iris
	Student, Pupil, Light, Gladioli, Novice	

102	pit excavation	source supply
	Colliery, Flaw, Mine, Start, Quarry	

Dual Meanings

Section 2 : Context Clue Sentences

Read the sentence and focus on the word that is underlined. Match this word with one of the answers below.

Questions:

1. I lost my pencil case, so I was feeling <u>down</u>.
    a. Unhappy
    b. At a lower level
    c. Soft, fine feathers

2. The old, comfortable cushion was filled with <u>down</u>.
    a. Unhappy
    b. At a lower level
    c. Soft, fine feathers

3. She bent <u>down</u> to pick up the kitten.
    a. Unhappy
    b. At a lower level
    c. Soft, fine feathers

4. It was late in the <u>evening</u> and he was very tired.
    a. Period of time at the end of the day
    b. Make or become even

5. It was <u>late</u> in the evening and he was very tired.
    a. Recently dead
    b. Arriving after the proper time
    c. Far on in the day/night

6. His father was <u>late</u> for the train.
    a. Recently dead
    b. Arriving after the proper time
    c. Far on in the day/night

7. Her <u>late</u> grandmother was the funniest person she had ever known.
    a. Recently dead
    b. Arriving after the proper time
    c. Far on in the day/night

Dual Meanings - Section 2

8. He was <u>evening</u> out the top of the cake with a spatula.
    a. Period of time at the end of the day
    b. Make or become even

9. The <u>sewer</u> was blocked with rubbish.
    a. An underground channel
    b. A person who joins or repairs with stitches.

10. She was a <u>sewer</u> for royalty.
    a. An underground channel
    b. A person who joins or repairs with stitches.

11. The splendid tapestry was of <u>fine</u> craftsmanship.
    a. Powdery or dusty
    b. Healthy
    c. Delicate or complex
    d. A sum of money paid as a punishment
    e. Bright and clear weather
    f. Satisfactory
    g. Thin thread or strand
    h. Prime quality

12. He paid the parking <u>fine</u>.
    a. Powdery or dusty
    b. Healthy
    c. Delicate or complex
    d. A sum of money paid as a punishment
    e. Bright and clear weather
    f. Satisfactory
    g. Thin thread or strand
    h. Prime quality

13. As the day was <u>fine</u> she hung out the washing.
    a. Powdery or dusty
    b. Healthy
    c. Delicate or complex
    d. A sum of money paid as a punishment
    e. Bright and clear weather
    f. Satisfactory
    g. Thin thread or strand
    h. Prime quality

Dual Meanings - Section 2

14. Grandmother had lots of hair which was wispy and <u>fine</u>.
    a. Powdery or dusty
    b. Healthy
    c. Delicate or complex
    d. A sum of money paid as a punishment
    e. Bright and clear weather
    f. Satisfactory
    g. Thin thread or strand
    h. Prime quality

15. I feel <u>fine</u> after my sudden illness.
    a. Powdery or dusty
    b. Healthy
    c. Delicate or complex
    d. A sum of money paid as a punishment
    e. Bright and clear weather
    f. Satisfactory
    g. Thin thread or strand
    h. Prime quality

16. The elaborate stitches on the cloak were <u>fine</u>.
    a. Powdery or dusty
    b. Healthy
    c. Delicate or complex
    d. A sum of money paid as a punishment
    e. Bright and clear weather
    f. Satisfactory
    g. Thin thread or strand
    h. Prime quality

17. The biscuits were crushed for the recipe until they were <u>fine.</u>
    a. Powdery or dusty
    b. Healthy
    c. Delicate or complex
    d. A sum of money paid as a punishment
    e. Bright and clear weather
    f. Satisfactory
    g. Thin thread or strand
    h. Prime quality

Dual Meanings - Section 2

18. "We can do it another day, that's <u>fine</u>".
    a. Powdery or dusty
    b. Healthy
    c. Delicate or complex
    d. A sum of money paid as a punishment
    e. Bright and clear weather
    f. Satisfactory
    g. Thin thread or strand
    h. Prime quality

19. He was about to <u>tear</u> down the old chimney.
    a. Destroy
    b. A drop of salty liquid
    c. Move very quickly
    d. To rip a hole or split

20. She was late and had to <u>tear</u> down the road.
    a. Destroy
    b. A drop of salty liquid
    c. Move very quickly
    d. To rip a hole or split

21. A silent <u>tear</u> fell down their face.
    a. Destroy
    b. A drop of salty liquid
    c. Move very quickly
    d. To rip a hole or split

22. There was a <u>tear</u> in her school trousers, again.
    a. Destroy
    b. A drop of salty liquid
    c. Move very quickly
    d. To rip a hole or split

23. The happy cat was <u>content</u> with her life.
    a. The things that are contained in something
    b. Satisfied
    c. Subject matter

Dual Meanings - Section 2

24. He was told that the <u>contents</u> of his sausage were completely vegetarian.
    a. The things that are contained in something
    b. Satisfied
    c. Subject matter

25. The <u>content</u> of the essay was easily understood.
    a. The things that are contained in something
    b. Satisfied
    c. Subject matter

26. When playing "Snap" the cards need to <u>match</u>.
    a. A short thin stick that ignites
    b. Correspond or fit with something
    c. An event where people compete

27. The two teams played in the <u>match</u>.
    a. A short thin stick that ignites
    b. Correspond or fit with something
    c. An event where people compete

28. She started to strike the <u>match</u>.
    a. A short thin stick that ignites
    b. Correspond or fit with something
    c. An event where people compete

29. The builders went on <u>strike</u>.
    a. Hit something with force
    b. Refuse to work as a protest
    c. Rub a match against a rough surface

30. He began to <u>strike</u> the drum, loudly.
    a. Hit something with force
    b. Refuse to work as a protest
    c. Rub a match against a rough surface

31. She started to <u>strike</u> the match.
    a. Hit something with force
    b. Refuse to work as a protest
    c. Rub a match against a rough surface

Dual Meanings - Section 2

32. It was a <u>novel</u> way of making his fortune.
    a. Innovative or original
    b. A true story
    c. A fictional story

33. The <u>novel</u> was about an imaginary land of flying cats and dogs.
    a. Innovative or original
    b. A true story
    c. A fictional story

34. As she sat for so long her leg got <u>number</u> and <u>number</u>.
    a. A song or a dance
    b. Quality or value
    c. Deader

35. He fastened the board with a <u>nail</u>.
    a. Small metal spike with a flat head
    b. Thin hard layer covering the finger or toe

36. The lady broke her <u>nail</u> when she opened the jar.
    a. Small metal spike with a flat head
    b. Thin hard layer covering the finger or toe

37. He used to <u>polish</u> the staircase.
    a. Improve a skill
    b. The language from Poland
    c. Buff or burnish

38. She began to <u>polish</u> up her dancing moves.
    a. Improve a skill
    b. The language from Poland
    c. Buff or burnish

39. He began to speak <u>Polish</u>.
    a. Improve a skill
    b. The language from Poland
    c. Buff or burnish

Dual Meanings - Section 2

40. He started to <u>park</u> his car near the park.
    a. Leave a vehicle somewhere
    b. A large public garden
    c. An area used for a particular purpose.

41. He started to park his car near the <u>park</u>.
    a. Leave a vehicle somewhere
    b. A large public garden
    c. An area used for a particular purpose.

42. They were so excited when they visited the theme <u>park</u>.
    a. Leave a vehicle somewhere
    b. A large public garden
    c. An area used for a particular purpose.

43. The children were hoping their mother would let them <u>pet</u> a pet.
    a. An animal or bird kept for pleasure
    b. A person treated with special favour
    c. To stoke or pat an animal.

44. The children were hoping their mother would let them pet a <u>pet</u>.
    a. An animal or bird kept for pleasure
    b. A person treated with special favour
    c. To stoke or pat an animal.

45. They called him the teacher's <u>pet</u>.
    a. An animal or bird kept for pleasure
    b. A person treated with special favour
    c. To stoke or pat an animal.

46. They were so happy to be in the <u>play</u>.
    a. To amuse yourself
    b. To participate in games
    c. A piece of writing performed by actors
    d. Perform on a musical instrument

47. She started to <u>play</u> the most beautiful melody.
    a. To amuse yourself
    b. To participate in games
    c. A piece of writing performed by actors
    d. Perform on a musical instrument

Dual Meanings - Section 2

48. The hockey players began to <u>play</u> with great gusto.

    a. To amuse yourself
    b. To participate in games
    c. A piece of writing performed by actors
    d. Perform on a musical instrument

49. The toddler began to <u>play</u> with his mum's keys.

    a. To amuse yourself
    b. To participate in games
    c. A piece of writing performed by actors
    d. Perform on a musical instrument

50. It was at that <u>point</u> when the archer started to point at the point of his arrow.

    a. Tapered, sharp end of a tool or weapon
    b. Particular place or moment
    c. Direct attention by extending a finger

51. It was at that point when the archer started to <u>point</u> at the point of his arrow.

    a. Tapered, sharp end of a tool or weapon
    b. Particular place or moment
    c. Direct attention by extending a finger

52. It was at that point when the archer started to point at the <u>point</u> of his arrow.

    a. Tapered, sharp end of a tool or weapon
    b. Particular place or moment
    c. Direct attention by extending a finger

53. He caught the <u>perch</u> with a rod.

    a. A freshwater fish with a spiny fin
    b. A high or narrow seat or resting place
    c. A branch, bar or ledge where birds roost

54. After the long climb the mountaineers found their <u>perch</u>.

    a. A freshwater fish with a spiny fin
    b. A high or narrow seat or resting place
    c. A branch, bar or ledge where birds roost

Dual Meanings - Section 2

55. After the long day the chickens found their <u>perch</u>.
    a. A freshwater fish with a spiny fin
    b. A high or narrow seat or resting place
    c. A branch, bar or ledge where birds roost

56. The plumber pulled out the <u>plug</u>.
    a. An electrical socket
    b. Promoting a product or event
    c. A thing that blocks a hole

57. The publisher began to <u>plug</u> his new book.
    a. An electrical socket
    b. Promoting a product or event
    c. A thing that blocks a hole

58. She had to put the <u>plug</u> into the wall.
    a. An electrical connector
    b. Promoting a product or event
    c. A thing that blocks a hole

59. He liked to <u>poach</u> the fresh fish with vegetables.
    a. Hunt game or catch fish illegally from private or protected areas
    b. Cook in a small amount of liquid

60. She liked to <u>poach</u> the animals from the game reserve.
    a. Hunt game or catch fish illegally from private or protected areas
    b. Cook in a small amount of liquid

61. She was on a winning <u>streak</u>.
    a. A long thin mark
    b. A period of success or luck
    c. Move very fast

62. There was a <u>streak</u> across the window.
    a. A long thin mark
    b. A period of success or luck
    c. Move very fast

Dual Meanings - Section 2

63. The cat began to <u>streak</u> across the busy street.
    a. A long thin mark
    b. A period of success or luck
    c. Move very fast

64. The tailor began to <u>tailor</u> the suit to fit the very tall man.
    a. A person who makes men's clothes
    b. To make clothes fit an individual
    c. To make or adapt for a particular purpose or person

65. The <u>tailor</u> began to tailor the suit to fit the very tall man.
    a. A person who makes men's clothes
    b. To make clothes fit an individual
    c. To make or adapt for a particular purpose or person

66. She could <u>tailor</u> her piano lessons to students of all ability.
    a. A person who makes men's clothes
    b. To make clothes fit an individual
    c. To make or adapt for a particular purpose or person

67. She began to <u>brush</u> her hair.
    a. A slight brief touch
    b. The bushy tail of a fox
    c. An act of brushing
    d. Perfect or enhance
    e. Small trees or shrubs

68. She felt the fox <u>brush</u> quickly past her.
    a. A slight brief touch
    b. The bushy tail of a fox
    c. An act of brushing
    d. Perfect or enhance
    e. Small trees or shrubs

69. The fox hid in the <u>brush</u>.
    a. A slight brief touch
    b. The bushy tail of a fox
    c. An act of brushing
    d. Perfect or enhance
    e. Small trees or shrubs

Dual Meanings - Section 2

70. He liked to <u>brush</u> up on his French.
    a. A slight brief touch
    b. The bushy tail of a fox
    c. An act of brushing
    d. Perfect or enhance
    e. Small trees or shrubs

71. The <u>bars</u> on the window kept out any intruders.
    a. To obstruct or hinder
    b. Rigid piece of wood or metal
    c. A tavern or inn

72. There were many rowdy <u>bars</u> in the town.
    a. To obstruct or hinder
    b. Rigid piece of wood or metal
    c. A tavern or inn

73. I was to <u>bar</u> her from entering the room.
    a. To obstruct or hinder
    b. Rigid piece of wood or metal
    c. A tavern or inn

74. She used the <u>colon</u> before a list of items in her writing.
    a. Main part of the large intestine
    b. Punctuation

75. The trainee doctors learnt about the <u>colon</u>.
    a. Main part of the large intestine
    b. Punctuation

76. She was a film <u>buff</u> who went to the cinema every week.
    a. A yellow/beige colour
    b. Polish with a soft cloth
    c. A person who knows a lot about a particular subject

77. Grandmother began to <u>buff</u> the furniture.
    a. A yellow/beige colour
    b. Polish with a soft cloth
    c. A person who knows a lot about a particular subject

Dual Meanings - Section 2

78. He took a small <u>buff</u> envelope from his pocket.
    a. A yellow/beige colour
    b. Polish with a soft cloth
    c. A person who knows a lot about a particular subject

79. His older brother caught the collecting <u>bug</u>.
    a. Small insect
    b. Microphone use for secret recording
    c. A germ or an illness
    d. An error in a computer program
    e. Enthusiasm for something

80. He found that the <u>bug</u> had corrupted all files.
    a. Small insect
    b. Microphone use for secret recording
    c. A germ or an illness
    d. An error in a computer program
    e. Enthusiasm for something

81. He found the <u>bug</u> planted on his phone.
    a. Small insect
    b. Microphone use for secret recording
    c. A germ or an illness
    d. An error in a computer program
    e. Enthusiasm for something

82. The stomach <u>bug</u> made him feel dreadful.
    a. Small insect
    b. Microphone use for secret recording
    c. A germ or an illness
    d. An error in a computer program
    e. Enthusiasm for something

Dual Meanings

Section 3 : Sentence Dictionary Definitions

Read both of the sentences and find one word in the set of answers that fits with both of these definitions.

Questions:

	1. Find a word that means: • An inflamed swelling • When a liquid reaches a temperature where it bubbles and turns to vapour
a.	Spruce
b.	Calf
c.	Rebel
d.	Boil
e.	Transport

	2. Find a word that means: • The fleshy part at the back of a person's leg • A young animal e.g. elephant or cow
a.	Spruce
b.	Calf
c.	Rebel
d.	Boil
e.	Transport

Dual Meanings - Section 3

3. Find a word that means:
   - An evergreen tree with hanging cones
   - Neat and smart

a.	Spruce
b.	Calf
c.	Rebel
d.	Boil
e.	Transport

4. Find a word that means:
   - A large vehicle, ship or aircraft carrying troops or stores
   - Carry people or goods from one place to another

a.	Spruce
b.	Calf
c.	Rebel
d.	Boil
e.	Transport

5. Find a word that means:
   - Refuse to obey the government or ruler
   - A mutineer

a.	Spruce
b.	Calf
c.	Rebel
d.	Boil
e.	Transport

Dual Meanings - Section 3

6. Find a word that means:
   - An illness or disease
   - Untidiness

a.	Stump
b.	Truffle
c.	Weight
d.	Disorder
e.	Beat

7. Find a word that means:
   - Baffle or perplex
   - Part of a tree trunk

a.	Stump
b.	Truffle
c.	Weight
d.	Disorder
e.	Beat

8. Find a word that means:
   - To thrash or pound
   - Pulse or vibration

a.	Stump
b.	Truffle
c.	Weight
d.	Disorder
e.	Beat

Dual Meanings - Section 3

9. Find a word that means:
- An underground fungus that is eaten as a delicacy
- A soft chocolate sweet

a.	Stump
b.	Truffle
c.	Weight
d.	Disorder
e.	Beat

10. Find a word that means:
- Mass or heaviness of a person or thing
- A burden, worry or load

a.	Stump
b.	Truffle
c.	Weight
d.	Disorder
e.	Beat

11. Find a word that means:
- Hit a golf ball gently into or near a hole
- Move something into a particular position

a.	Address
b.	Putting
c.	Cross
d.	Live
e.	Buffet

Dual Meanings - Section 3

12. Find a word that means:	
• A formal speech • Think about a task and begin to deal with it	
a.	Address
b.	Putting
c.	Cross
d.	Live
e.	Buffet

13. Find a word that means:	
• Repeatedly struck by wind or waves • Meal made up of several dishes you serve yourself	
a.	Address
b.	Putting
c.	Cross
d.	Live
e.	Buffet

14. Find a word that means:	
• A mixture of two things • A mark, object or shape formed by two intersecting lines or pieces	
a.	Address
b.	Putting
c.	Cross
d.	Live
e.	Buffet

Dual Meanings - Section 3

15. Find a word that means:
- Make one's home in a particular place
- Connected to a source of electric current

a.	Address
b.	Putting
c.	Cross
d.	Live
e.	Buffet

16. Find a word that means:
- To take out or remove
- Using colours and shapes (in art) to create an effect rather than attempting to represent real life accurately

a.	Compress
b.	Tables
c.	Compact
d.	Abstract
e.	Proceeds

17. Find a word that means:
- Squeeze or press two things together
- A pad pressed on to part of the body to relieve inflammation or stop bleeding

a.	Compress
b.	Tables
c.	Compact
d.	Abstract
e.	Proceeds

Dual Meanings - Section 3

18. Find a word that means:
- Money obtained from an event or activity
- To carry on or continue

a.	Compress
b.	Tables
c.	Compact
d.	Abstract
e.	Proceeds

19. Find a word that means:
- A small flat case that contains face powder and a mirror
- Closely and neatly packed together

a.	Compress
b.	Tables
c.	Compact
d.	Abstract
e.	Proceeds

20. Find a word that means:
- A set of facts or figures arranged in rows and columns
- Multiplication sums arranged in sets

a.	Compress
b.	Tables
c.	Compact
d.	Abstract
e.	Proceeds

Section 4 : Homograph Word Banks

Match each of the five words in the word bank to the five clues.

Question 1

> rose   fox   moped
>
> fly   number

Choose one word from the word bank that means:

a. A quality or value
   A song
   Lacking sensation

b. To baffle or deceive
   An animal with a pointed muzzle

c. A soft pink colour
   A cap with holes on a shower, hose or spout
   A flower
   Past tense of rise

d. Listless and gloomy
   A motorcycle with a small engine

e. To move quickly
   Move quickly through the air
   Control an aircraft
   Insect with transparent wings
   Displayed on a flagpole

Dual Meanings - Section 4

Question 2

> quarry ship present
>
> page clip

Choose one word from the word bank that means:

a. Flexible or spring-loaded device for holding objects
   Cut or trim
   Hit quickly or lightly

b. Existing in a particular place
   Tense of a verb
   Formally introduce someone to someone else
   Introduce and take part in a show
   Give someone something, formally

c. A large vessel or craft
   To deliver or send

d. A young boy who attends a bride at a wedding
   A young boy or man who runs errands in a hotel
   A young boy training to be a knight
   One sheet of paper
   A section of data displayed on a computer screen

e. A person or animal that is being chased or hunted
   A place where materials are dug up out of the earth

Question 3

> permit   capital   compound
>
> bar   tie

Choose one word from the word bank that means:

a. To forbid or prevent
   A short unit in music
   Long rigid piece of wood or metal etc.
   A counter in a public house

b. Large letter
   Top part of a pillar
   The most important city or town in a country or region
   Wealth that is owned, lent or borrowed

c. Make something possible
   To say that someone is allowed to do something
   An official document that allows someone to do something or go somewhere

d. Attach or fasten
   Restrict to a particular place
   Connect or link
   Achieve the same score
   Strip of material that is worn

e. A thing made of two or more elements
   A large open area enclosed by a fence

Dual Meanings - Section 4

Question 4

> fast   date   frequent
>
> invalid   letter

Choose one word from the word bank that means:

a. Ill
   Void
   False

b. Character, sign or symbol
   Message

c. Appointment
   Day
   Partner like a girlfriend or boyfriend
   Age
   Go out with
   Fruit

d. Recurrent
   Visit or spend time in

e. Speedy
   Swift
   Secure
   Loyal
   Eat nothing

Question 5

> present   produce   punch
>
> read   ruler

Choose one word from the word bank that means:

a. Discover information
   Look at and comprehend meaning

b. Make, manufacture or create
   Things that have been grown
   Supervise the making of a musical recording

c. A strip of rigid material marked with measurements
   A person who has authority and control over a people or country

d. Existing or happening now
   Formally introduce someone to someone else
   Produce a show or broadcast for the public
   A gift

e. A drink made with wine, fruit and spices
   To pierce a hole in something
   A blow with the fist
   Press a button or key on a machine

Dual Meanings - Section 4

Question 6

> leaves   ring   stalk
>
> second   scale

Choose one word from the word bank that means:

a. A group of people with a shared goal or interest
   A circular band, object or mark
   A loud, clear sound or tone
   An enclosed space where a performance, sport or show takes place

b. To go away from
   Plural of flat green part of a plant that is attached to the stem

c. A hard deposit that forms on teeth
   An arrangement of notes in order of pitch
   An instrument for weighing
   Overlapping plates protecting reptiles or fish
   A range of values forming a system for measuring or grading something

d. Walk in a proud, stiff or angry way
   Stem of a plant
   Follow stealthily

e. Support a nomination before
   Lower in position
   Ordinal number
   A unit of time equal to one sixtieth of a minute
   A very short time

Question 7

> saw   spring   toast
>
> trip   watch

Choose one word from the word bank that means:

a. A person who is greatly respected or admired
Sliced bread that has been browned and is now crisp
An act of raising glasses at a gathering and drinking together in honour of a person or thing

b. To look at attentively
Be cautious about
Keep under careful observation
A shift worked by firefighters or police officers
A small clock worn on a strap on your wrist

c. To catch your foot on something and stumble or fall
A journey to a place and back again
Walk, run or dance in quick, light steps

d. Become aware with the eyes. Past tense
A tool with a long and thin jagged blade

e. A spiral metal coil
A place where water wells up from underground
The season after winter
A sudden jump upwards or forwards

Question 8

> commune   left   chest
>
> sign   right

Choose one word from the word bank that means:

- a. A signal
  An indication that something exists
  Each of the 12 divisions of the zodiac

- b. A large strong box for storing or transporting things
  Upper body or torso

- c. Justified or morally good
  Precise and valid
  Correct or make up for a wrong
  A thing which is to the East, if you are facing North

- d. A thing which is to the West, if you are facing North
  Past participle of leave

- e. A group of people living together and sharing possessions
  Share your intimate thoughts or feelings with

Dual Meanings - Section 4

Question 9

> spoke   wave   can
>
> clear   patch

Choose one word from the word bank that means:

a. Ridge of water moving along the surface of the sea
   A slightly curling lock of hair
   A regular to-and-fro motion of particles of matter involved in transmitting either heat, light or sound

b. Smudge, smear or stain
   A small plot of land
   A piece of material used to mend a hole

c. Each of the rods connecting the centre of a wheel to its rim
   Past tense of speak

d. Free from guilt or disease
   Transparent
   Easy to see, hear or understand
   Make people leave a place

e. To be able to
   To be allowed to
   Cylindrical metal container

Question 10

> save   troll   sink
>
> quail   key

Choose one word from the word bank that means:

a. Feel or show fear
   Short-tailed game bird

b. Word or system for solving a code
   A small piece of shaped metal inserted into a lock
   Buttons on a panel for operating a computer or typewriter
   Group of notes making up a scale

c. Move in a casual and unhurried way
   A ugly giant or dwarf in a story

d. Put money or resources into
   Go to the bottom of the sea
   Gradually decrease in amount or strength
   Fixed basin with a water supply and drainage pipe

e. Store or keep for further use
   Except
   Prevent someone from dying
   Store data. Computing
   Rescue or prevent from harm or danger

Question 11

> yard   crane   splash
>
> stall   tick

Choose one word from the word bank that means:

a. Fall in scattered drops
Bright patch of colour
Small quantity of liquid added to a drink
Prominently display a story or photograph in a newspaper or magazine

b. A regular short, sharp sound
Tiny insect-like creature that sucks blood
A mark to show something is correct

c. A piece of enclosed ground next to a building
Unit of length equal to 3 feet
A long piece of wood that the sail of a ship hangs from

d. A wading bird with long legs and a long neck
A tall machine used for moving heavy objects

e. A compartment for an animal in a stable or cowshed
A compartment in a set of toilets
A seat in the choir of a church
When an engine suddenly stops running
The ground floor seats in a theatre
A stand where goods are sold in a market

Dual Meanings - Section 4

Question 12

> spin   passage   jumper
>
> run   back

Choose one word from the word bank that means:

a. Take someone somewhere in a car
   Continue, operate or proceed
   To publish a story in a newspaper
   Move at a speed faster than a walk
   A ladder in stockings or tights
   A journey or route

b. Turn around quickly
   A brief trip in a vehicle for pleasure
   A spinning motion
   Draw out and twist fibres of wool or cotton to convert them into yarn

c. A sweater or pullover
   A person or animal that jumps

d. A short section of a book, document or musical work
   Journey by sea or air
   A way through or across something

e. Defending a player in a team game
   So as to return to an earlier or normal position or state
   Into the past
   Give support to
   Cover the back of an object
   Upper part of an animal's body

Question 13

> blossom   does   pitcher
>
> till   park

Choose one word from the word bank that means:

a. A large public garden in a town
A large area of land attached to a country house
To leave a vehicle somewhere for a time

b. Female deer or reindeer. Plural
3rd person singular present of do
Female of a rabbit or hare. Plural

c. A large jug
Someone throwing a ball in a game of baseball

d. Become strong and healthy
A flower or mass of flowers on a tree

e. A cash register or drawer for money
Prepare and cultivate land for crops

Question 14

> right   contest   suit
>
> progress   thrust

Choose one word from the word bank that means:

- a. Push suddenly or violently
  The main point of an argument
  The force produced by an engine to push forward a jet or rocket

- b. Be right for someone's features or figure
  A set of clothes made from the same fabric
  A set of cards

- c. Challenge or dispute a decision or theory
  Take part in a competition or election
  An event in which people compare to see who is the best

- d. Correct or satisfactory
  To put something back in a normal or upright position
  Factually correct
  On or to the right side

- e. To move forwards towards a place
  To improve or develop

Question 15

> recall   bark   wave
>
> retire   level

Choose one word from the word bank that means:

a. Go to bed
   Leave your job and stop working
   Withdraw from a race or match because of accident or injury

b. A slightly curling lock of hair
   A gesture or signal made by moving your hand
   Move to and fro with a swaying motion
   A ridge of water moving along the surface of the sea

c. The tough covering of the trunk and branches of a tree
   The sharp sudden cry of a dog, fox or seal
   To say a command or question suddenly or fiercely

d. Remember
   Ask for faulty products to be returned
   To call again

e. A horizontal line or surface
   Steady, even, regular or constant
   Position on a scale
   Particular floor of a building

Question 16

> apply   fawn   mellow
>
> point   view

Choose one word from the word bank that means:

a. Relaxed and good humoured
   Pleasantly smooth or soft in sound, taste or colour

b. A unit of scoring
   A particular place or moment
   The purpose of something
   A small dot used as punctuation or in decimals
   Directions marked on a compass
   Junction of two railway lines
   Aim or indicate in a particular direction

c. Put a substance on a surface
   Be relevant
   Make a formal request for something
   Bring into operation or use

d. A young deer
   A light brown colour
   To try and please someone by flattering them or being too attentive

e. An attitude or opinion
   Look at or inspect
   Something seen from a particular position, especially natural scenery

Dual Meanings

Answers

Section 1 : 2-Section Dictionary Definitions

Q	A	Q	A	Q	A	Q	A
1	Tap	27	Express	53	Bank	79	Mouth
2	Dash	28	Counter	54	Page	80	Leaf
3	Stem	29	Cape	55	Tip	81	Record
4	Wind	30	Angle	56	Stall	82	Deck
5	Yard	31	Toll	57	Race	83	Gross
6	Ball	32	Note	58	Lean	84	Row
7	Incense	33	Stick	59	Hatch	85	Beef
8	Loom	34	Mind	60	Flag	86	Panel
9	Might	35	Knot	61	Pound	87	Staff
10	Carp	36	Bat	62	Mean	88	Train
11	Hail	37	Tick	63	Tuck	89	Skate
12	Nick	38	Shell	64	Well	90	Kind
13	Top	39	Jam	65	Pale	91	State
14	Mine	40	Habit	66	Object	92	Interest
15	Case	41	Entrance	67	Long	93	Plane
16	Cross	42	Firm	68	Rank	94	Desert
17	Rock	43	Caper	69	Jet	95	Stalk
18	Fast	44	Lap	70	Light	96	Type
19	Till	45	Grain	71	Bear	97	Punch
20	Palm	46	Utter	72	File	98	Pluck
21	Kid	47	Wound	73	Sound	99	Dog
22	Hawk	48	Sole	74	Skip	100	Ring
23	Lead	49	Peer	75	Volume	101	Pupil
24	Box	50	Organ	76	Bay	102	Mine
25	Season	51	Fair	77	Plain		
26	Hip	52	Flat	78	Bark		

Dual Meanings - Answers

Section 2 : Context-Clue Sentences

Q	A	Q	A	Q	A	Q	A
1	a	22	d	43	c	64	b
2	c	23	b	44	a	65	a
3	b	24	a	45	b	66	c
4	a	25	c	46	c	67	c
5	c	26	b	47	d	68	a
6	b	27	c	48	b	69	e
7	a	28	a	49	a	70	d
8	b	29	b	50	b	71	b
9	a	30	a	51	c	72	c
10	b	31	c	52	a	73	a
11	h	32	a	53	a	74	b
12	d	33	c	54	b	75	a
13	e	34	c	55	c	76	c
14	g	35	a	56	c	77	b
15	b	36	b	57	b	78	a
16	c	37	c	58	a	79	e
17	a	38	a	59	b	80	d
18	f	39	b	60	a	81	b
19	a	40	a	61	b	82	c
20	c	41	b	62	a		
21	b	42	c	63	c		

Section 3 : Sentence Dictionary Definitions

Q	A	Q	A	Q	A
1	d	8	e	15	d
2	b	9	b	16	d
3	a	10	c	17	a
4	e	11	b	18	e
5	c	12	a	19	c
6	d	13	e	20	b
7	a	14	c		

Dual Meanings - Answers

Section 4 : Homograph Word Banks

Q	A	Q	A	Q	A
1 a	number	7 a	toast	13 a	park
b	fox	b	watch	b	does
c	rose	c	trip	c	pitcher
d	moped	d	saw	d	blossom
e	fly	e	spring	e	till
2 a	clip	8 a	sign	14 a	thrust
b	present	b	chest	b	suit
c	ship	c	right	c	contest
d	page	d	left	d	right
e	quarry	e	commune	e	progress
3 a	bar	9 a	wave	15 a	retire
b	capital	b	patch	b	wave
c	permit	c	spoke	c	bark
d	tie	d	clear	d	recall
e	compound	e	can	e	level
4 a	invalid	10 a	quail	16 a	mellow
b	letter	b	key	b	point
c	date	c	troll	c	apply
d	frequent	d	sink	d	fawn
e	fast	e	save	e	view
5 a	read	11 a	splash		
b	produce	b	tick		
c	ruler	c	yard		
d	present	d	crane		
e	punch	e	stall		
6 a	ring	12 a	run		
b	leaves	b	spin		
c	scale	c	jumper		
d	stalk	d	passage		
e	second	e	back		

Printed in Great Britain
by Amazon